HOW? WHO? WHAT? WHEN? WHERE? WHY?

Questions
kids
ask

ABOUT
WEATHER

PUBLISHER	Joseph R. DeVarennes	
PUBLICATION DIRECTOR	Kenneth H. Pearson	
ADVISORS	Roger Aubin	
	Robert Furlonger	
EDITORIAL SUPERVISOR	Jocelyn Smyth	
PRODUCTION MANAGER	Ernest Homewood	
PRODUCTION ASSISTANTS	Martine Gingras	Kathy Kishimoto
	Catherine Gordon	Peter Thomlison
CONTRIBUTORS	Alison Dickie	Nancy Prasad
	Bill Ivy	Lois Rock
	Jacqueline Kendel	Merebeth Switzer
	Anne Langdon	Dave Taylor
	Sheila Macdonald	Alison Tharen
	Susan Marshall	Donna Thomson
	Pamela Martin	Pam Young
	Colin McCance	
SENIOR EDITOR	Robin Rivers	
EDITORS	Brian Cross	Ann Martin
	Anne Louise Mahoney	Mayta Tannenbaum
PUBLICATION ADMINISTRATOR	Anna Good	
ART AND DESIGN	Richard Comely	Ronald Migliore
	Robert B. Curry	Penelope Moir
	George Elliott	Marion Stuck
	Marilyn James	Bill Suddick
	Robert Johanssen	Sue Wilkinson

Canadian Cataloguing in Publication Data

Main entry under title:

Questions kids ask about weather.

(Questions kids ask ; 20)
ISBN 0-7172-2559-3

1. Weather—Miscellanea—Juvenile literature.
2. Meteorology—Miscellanea—Juvenile literature.
3. Children's questions and answers.
I. Smyth, Jocelyn.   II. Comely, Richard.   III. Series.

QC863.5.Q48 1988   j551.5   C89-093169-0

Questions Kids Ask . . . about WEATHER

continued

What is weather?

The weather is the way things are outside. The main ingredients of weather are water, wind and sun. These three things can create a snowstorm, a rainbow or a beautiful sunny day. Weather occurs in the layer of the atmosphere closest to the earth. Known as the troposphere, this layer is about 10 kilometres (6 miles) thick.

Since the weather has such a powerful impact on all aspects of our lives, people have been watching and studying weather for thousands of years.

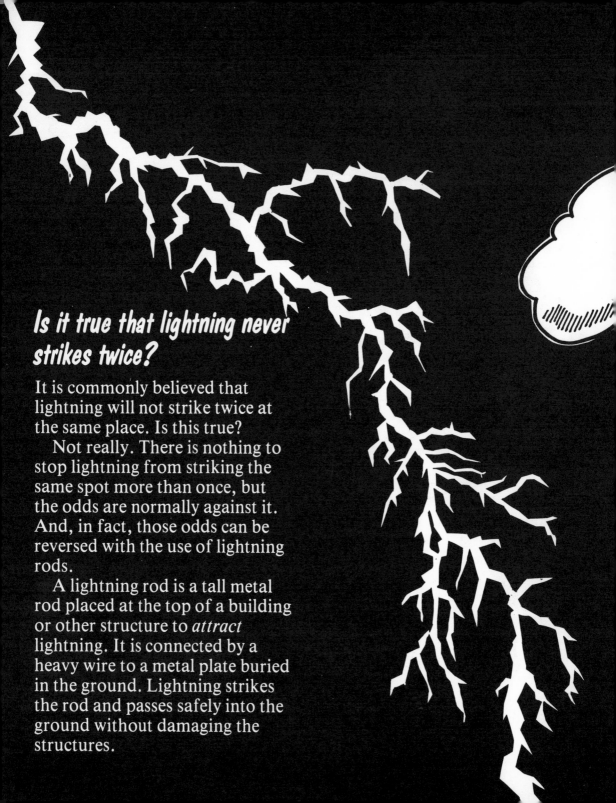

Is it true that lightning never strikes twice?

It is commonly believed that lightning will not strike twice at the same place. Is this true?

Not really. There is nothing to stop lightning from striking the same spot more than once, but the odds are normally against it. And, in fact, those odds can be reversed with the use of lightning rods.

A lightning rod is a tall metal rod placed at the top of a building or other structure to *attract* lightning. It is connected by a heavy wire to a metal plate buried in the ground. Lightning strikes the rod and passes safely into the ground without damaging the structures.

What is the safest place to be during a thunderstorm?

Because lightning strikes during a thunderstorm, it is very important to know where to go when a thunderstorm starts. It's best to be in a house or a large building because it's safe inside.

> DID YOU KNOW . . . as well as during thunderstorms, lightning may also occur during snowstorms, sand storms and in clouds over erupting volcanoes.

What is St. Elmo's fire?

St. Elmo's fire is a bluish glow that occasionally occurs during thunderstorms, snowstorms and dust storms. The glow of light is seen at the top of tall objects such as church steeples, trees and the wings of airplanes. It is a steady discharge of electricity that can only be seen at night. Often a crackling sound is heard along with it.

St. Elmo's fire was named after the patron saint of sailors, because mariners often spotted this glow at the top of their ships' masts.

However, while inside, keep away from water and electrical systems.

If you're outside, avoid standing under a lone tree since lightning is attracted by tall objects. Go into dense woods rather than staying in an open spot. Stay away from beaches, lakes and swimming pools since water may draw the lightning. Keep away from metal fences and buildings.

What is a chinook?

On the Prairies the winter is often bitterly cold. You have to bundle up to go outside: extra socks, warm boots, a long scarf, a snug hat and a heavy coat will keep you warm. Don't forget your mitts! It's freezing out there.

If you live less than 400 km (250 miles) east of the Rocky Mountains, however, you could get as many as 35 warm days in the middle of winter. What makes this happen? A chinook.

A chinook starts out as a warm, moist wind that blows east from the Pacific. As it passes over the Rocky Mountains, the moisture falls as rain or snow. The wind that reaches the land east of the Rockies is dry and very warm.

A chinook can raise the air temperature by over 25°C (45°F) in an hour!

8

DID YOU KNOW . . . this warm wind is named after the Chinook Indians of the Columbia River area, west of the Rocky Mountains.

Can people control the weather?

Wouldn't it be great if you could decide what the weather would be like!

You could ask for warm, sunny weather when you wanted to play outdoors or a little extra snow for those winter days when you really couldn't face going to school.

Through the ages, people have tried to influence the weather. So far, only cloud seeding has succeeded. In cloud seeding, an airplane sprays chemicals into the clouds so that their moisture quickly falls as rain or snow. During a long, dry summer, farmers might use cloud seeding to get rain for their crops.

This method of weather control has also been used to influence hailstorms and hurricanes by forcing the precipitation to fall before the storm becomes dangerous. Because scientists are still testing this application of cloud seeding, it is not done very often.

So until we learn more about it, the weather will continue to control us!

Why does the wind blow?

You know that you cannot stack water up at one end of the bath. Even if you try to push it to one end, it always flows back down.

Air flows in a similar way. For example, when the sun shines and heats air, the warm air rises. Immediately, cooler air from the side rushes in. This rushing air is the wind.

9

What does a barometer do?

Air is made of molecules of gas, water and dust. Molecules are tiny bits of matter. Everything is made up of matter—even you! The weight of the air pushing on the earth is called air pressure, and this is measured by a barometer.

You may have seen an *aneroid barometer*—it looks like a clock.

Instead of having the two hands of a clock, the barometer has a single needle which points to words that describe the weather. Inside the barometer, a mechanism measures the air pressure. Low pressure means that the weather will be rainy; high pressure indicates good weather.

A *mercury barometer* is a long glass tube with its open end in liquid mercury. As the air pressure changes, so does the level of mercury in the tube.

By keeping an eye on the barometer, you will know when the weather is going to change.

What does a weather vane do?

A weather vane has fixed rods that point north, south, east and west. Above them, an arrow swings in the wind. The arrow's point is thin, but its tail end is wide, allowing it to catch the breeze. The narrow tip of the arrow points into the wind, telling us which direction the wind is coming from.

Weather vanes are often placed on tall buildings and are sometimes made in fancy shapes. One popular design is the rooster.

DID YOU KNOW . . . in Britain, where a rooster is called a cock, the weather vane is also known as a weathercock.

What are weather balloons used for?

Surrounding the earth is a thick layer of air and gases called the atmosphere. Weather balloons carry various instruments such as thermometers, barometers to measure air pressure and hygrometers to measure humidity into the upper atmosphere.

Some weather balloons contain special foil reflectors that are tracked by radar down on the ground. Their purpose is to determine wind speed and direction. They are called rawinsondes ("ra" from *ra*dar and "win" from *win*ds).

Other balloons carry little electronic instruments called radiosondes which send radio signals to stations on the ground. They measure temperature, pressure and moisture.

When the balloons rise to a certain height, they burst and fall back to earth. They are designed to work that way because weather stations all over the world send up hundreds of thousands of weather balloons every year!

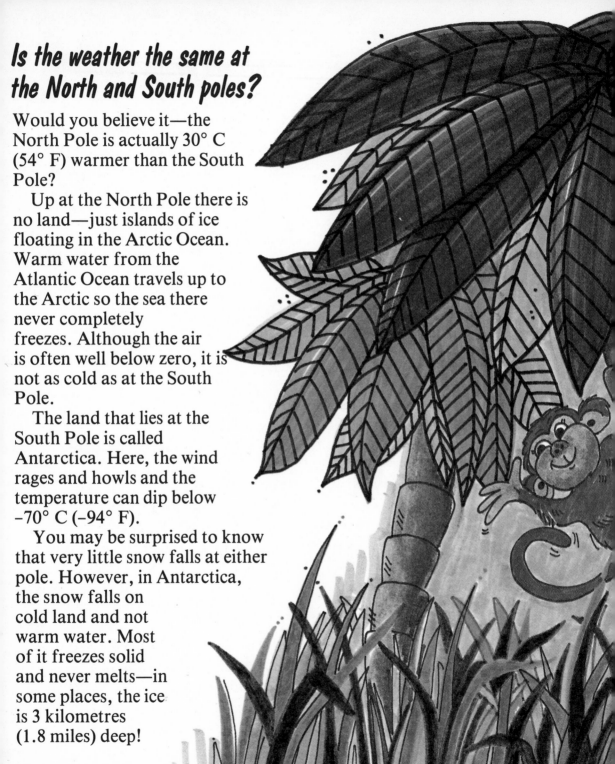

Is the weather the same at the North and South poles?

Would you believe it—the North Pole is actually 30° C (54° F) warmer than the South Pole?

Up at the North Pole there is no land—just islands of ice floating in the Arctic Ocean. Warm water from the Atlantic Ocean travels up to the Arctic so the sea there never completely freezes. Although the air is often well below zero, it is not as cold as at the South Pole.

The land that lies at the South Pole is called Antarctica. Here, the wind rages and howls and the temperature can dip below –70° C (–94° F).

You may be surprised to know that very little snow falls at either pole. However, in Antarctica, the snow falls on cold land and not warm water. Most of it freezes solid and never melts—in some places, the ice is 3 kilometres (1.8 miles) deep!

12

Does the Pacific Ocean affect west-coast weather?

The temperature of the Pacific Ocean affects the temperature of nearby places. Water warms very slowly in the sun, but when it is warm it takes a long time to cool down. The air around Vancouver and other coastal cities and towns is slow to heat up in the summer, so they never get as hot as other parts of Canada. In winter, the opposite happens. Because the sea takes a long time to cool down, the Pacific coast has a warmer winter than other areas of the country. As a result, the clouds drop their moisture as rain, not snow.

Places near the ocean get a lot of rain because the sun turns the seawater into water vapor, which rises and forms rain clouds.

DID YOU KNOW . . . the weather at the poles was not always cold. Millions of years ago, Antarctica was covered in forest like a tropical jungle.

WELCOME TO THE SOUTH POLE

What do meteorologists do?

A meteorologist is a scientist who studies the changes in our atmosphere that produce different kinds of weather. The meteorologist gathers information from land, sea and air by using thermometers, barometers, weather balloons, satellites, radar and a variety of computers. Not only can he or she predict the temperature or the possibility of precipitation (rain or snow), but, by studying complicated computer equations, the meteorologist can chart cloud patterns. This is a very important step in detecting tropical storms and hurricanes early enough to warn people of their danger.

Most of you have probably seen or heard weather forecasters report the weather on television or radio. But don't get them mixed up with meteorologists. Meteorologists usually work for government agencies, airlines and even space centers!

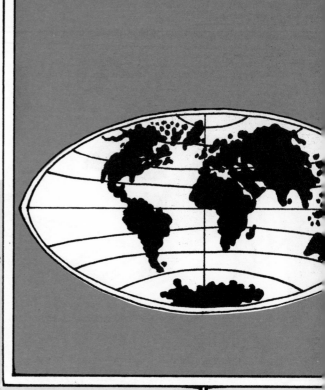

What is a monsoon?

A monsoon is a type of wind which changes direction from season to season. In a monsoon climate, a hot, dry season alternates with a season of heavy rain. Normally, the air over the land is heated by the sun. Ocean air is cooler. This heating and cooling affects the air currents far above the earth. These air

What are horse latitudes?

If you look at a globe of the world, you will notice many lines running across the surface. These are called lines of latitude and they are measured in degrees (°). The line of latitude that runs across the middle of the world is called the equator. It divides the globe in half. The regions 30° north and 30° south of the equator are known as the horse latitudes. The weather in this area is sunny and warm, and the winds are calm or very light.

The unpredictable winds once caused serious problems for sailors who depended on the wind to sail their ships across the ocean. If the ships were delayed very long, the sailors sometimes had to throw any horses they were carrying overboard to save water. It is thought that that may be how the region got its name, horse latitudes.

currents cause the reversal of the monsoon winds. In winter, the air is hot and dry as it moves over the land to the sea. In summer, hot, wet air blows in over the land from the sea. Clouds build up and the rains begin. Monsoon rains can be unbelievably heavy. Monsoons occur throughout Southern Asia, the most dramatic being in India.

Can the wind blow someone over?

You have probably been out in storms when it is hard to walk against the wind. When the wind is blowing at about 60 kilometres (40 miles) per hour—the speed that people drive cars in the city —everyone finds it hard to keep moving.

When the wind reaches speeds of over 100 kilometres (60 miles) per hour, people can be blown over and trees uprooted! In stronger winds, a person may even be carried up into the air, and that is very dangerous. Hurricanes and tornadoes often have winds this strong.

The strongest winds ever recorded were at Mount Washington in New Hampshire. On April 12, 1934, one gust blew at 372 kilometres (231 miles) per hour—the speed at which some aircraft fly!

What is a jet stream?

Until high-altitude aircraft were built and used during World War II, meteorologists didn't know that jet streams existed. At that time pilots discovered that the speed of their aircraft could drop by as much as 320 kilometres (200 miles) per hour. They were flying into the strong winds of the jet stream, located 9140 metres (30 000 feet) above the earth.

What are the doldrums?

The doldrums are a region of the ocean near the equator known for slow currents, long spells of calm air and heavy rains. The name *doldrums* means listlessness or lack of energy. Sailors used this term to describe both the area where their ships were often stalled for weeks and the way they felt as they waited for winds to blow.

We still talk about people being "in the doldrums," meaning that they are feeling dull and depressed.

DID YOU KNOW . . . jets ride on the winds that blow high above the earth. Computers on board tell them how high to fly to get the best winds.

Studies soon showed that these high-altitude westerly winds blow at 160 to 400 kilometres (100 to 250 miles) per hour. The speed and path of the jet stream winds depend on the seasons and the lower-level winds. In the winter the wind speed is high and in the summer it is lower.

In North America, the general path of the 480-kilometre (300-mile) wide jet stream is from Alaska, flowing south over the Rocky Mountains to the state of Kansas, then curving back north to the Great Lakes before heading east to the Atlantic Ocean.

When traveling with the jet stream on a trip from New York to London, a trans-Atlantic jet can reach much higher speeds than when going in the opposite direction.

Can looking at snow make you blind?

Snow blindness is a temporary dimming or loss of sight caused by light reflected off snow. If you look at light reflected off snow for a long period of time, you could become blind. Just as we are careful about looking at the sun, we should be cautious about the glare reflected off snow.

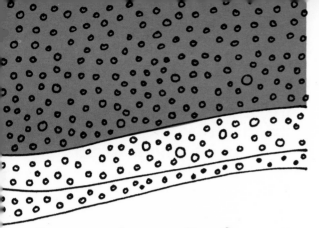

Is snow always white?

When snowflakes fall through the atmosphere, they hit all sorts of impurities in the air, including dust, soot and pollen. Sometimes the dust particles are so thick that they actually color the snow. When this happens, the snowflakes look dirty.

This process helps wash impurities from the air. It's been estimated that a snowfall lasting several days in a large industrial city will wash tons of solid impurities from the air.

DID YOU KNOW . . .
10 centimetres
(4 inches) of snow melts
down to about 1
centimetre (0.4 inches)
of water.

1 cm

Do all snowflakes look alike?

Each snowflake is formed in a cloud by several tiny ice crystals. The crystals can form an infinite number of beautiful forms of snowflakes.

There are 78 snowflake types identified by the meteorologists who study snowfalls. Each type may have any number of variations. Perfectly symmetrical snowflakes are uncommon. Scientists try to classify snowflake types to learn to accurately predict snowfalls. They want to identify snowflake types that may cause avalanches or conditions in the clouds that might cause hail to fall, ruining farm crops.

The shape of snowflakes can change while they are falling. The snowflake may be covered by water crystals in clouds or water vapor in the air. It may join with other snowflakes or be broken up by the wind before reaching the ground. Although scientists can classify types of snowflakes, they admit that they have never seen two identical snowflakes.

What causes floods?

Floods are caused by heavy rains, spring thaws or huge ocean waves created by storms, earthquakes, volcanoes or high winds.

Serious floods are caused by long periods of heavy rain. The rain runs off into the nearest stream, which carries it to the river. Eventually, the river rises so high that it overflows its banks and floods the surrounding land. In many countries where people live crowded along great rivers, governments are working to control the rivers.

Spring can bring flooding to areas where there is a lot of snow, as melting snow and ice cause rivers to overflow.

Floods also come from the ocean, and from lakes as well. Great storms can drive huge waves against the shore, piling up the water until it drowns low-lying land along the coast. This has always been a great problem in the Netherlands, where much of the land is below sea level. The Dutch have built dikes and huge storm barriers to prevent flooding.

Floods are not always bad, however. The annual flooding of the Nile River in Egypt helps to irrigate the Nile Valley. This allows people to grow crops in an area that would otherwise be a desert.

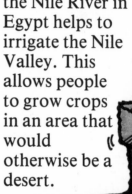

Which places have the greatest and least amount of rainfall?

Tutunendo in Colombia, South America, has an average of 11 770 millimetres (463 inches) of rain each year. If the water was not absorbed by the ground, there would be enough to cover a two-storey house.

Too wet for you? Well, don't move to the town of Cherrapunji in the mountains of northern India. Cherrapunji always has a lot of rain, but in freak years it can be even worse than Tutunendo. It once had 890 millimetres (35 inches) of rain in a 24-hour period!

Meanwhile, in the desert called Desierto de Atacama in Chile, South America, it almost never rains. There was a dry spell there that lasted about 400 years. It hasn't rained since 1971. As you can imagine, not too many plants grow there.

DID YOU KNOW . . . between August, 1860 and July, 1861, 2644 centimetres (1041 inches) of rain fell on Cherrapunji.

What is a waterspout?

When you drink water through a straw, you suck the air out of the straw and the water rushes up to take its place. Waterspouts, which happen mostly in tropical regions, are formed in a similar way.

Hot air always rises above cold air, and when the weather is very warm the hot air rises quickly. Cooler air rushes into the gap. When this happens over a lake or ocean, the wind can whip the water into a twisting column, much the way water is sucked up a straw.

Sometimes small fish are carried up in the waterspout and may later fall down with the rain!

DID YOU KNOW . . . the tallest waterspout ever was in New South Wales, Australia, on May 16, 1898. It was over 1500 metres (4950 feet) high.

What is a hurricane?

Hurricanes are violent storms that form over tropical seas. They have winds of at least 118 kilometres (73 miles) per hour. The winds blow in a circular motion, counter-clockwise above the equator and clockwise below the equator.

Hurricanes can be different sizes—some may be only about 40 kilometres (25 miles) across, but others can be from 150 kilometres (93 miles) to 950 kilometres (590 miles) across.

At the center of the hurricane is a small area of calm called the eye of the storm. All around the eye, the rain pours down and terrible winds blow. These winds whip up huge waves in the ocean, uproot palm trees on tropical islands, and flatten homes.

Because the hurricane needs the energy of the warm sea to sustain itself, it loses its force as it moves over land. Hurricanes eventually blow themselves out, becoming simple tropical storms. Using radar and satellites, meteorologists are able to watch a hurricane and warn people of the storm's approach.

DID YOU KNOW . . .
hurricane, cyclone and typhoon are words used in different parts of the world to describe the same type of storm. In Australia, these tropical storms are called willy-willies!

Why are hurricanes given names?

Each season, the scientists who watch for hurricanes make up a list of names in alphabetical order. The first hurricane of the season is given a name beginning with A, the next with B, and so on through the alphabet. The scientists use these names to help them tell one hurricane from another and to warn people about which one is approaching.

How many different kinds of clouds are there?

When you look up at the clouds, what shapes do you see? Maybe you see dragons, alligators or even a herd of elephants.

Scientists also look at the shapes of clouds and give them names to match. They use Latin words for names. *Stratus* means "covering" and it describes flat dense clouds. *Cumulus* means "heap." Cumulus clouds look like heaps of cotton balls. *Cirrus* means "curl"—these wispy white clouds look like curly hair. *Nimbus,* which means "rain cloud," describes a cloud that is full of water.

Scientists use these words in different combinations to describe high clouds, low clouds and the clouds in between. They can tell which ones are likely to bring rain or snow, and which ones are going to float away.

DID YOU KNOW . . . the dark, towering clouds you see during a thunderstorm are called cumulonimbus. You can see that the word means "a puffy cloud that brings rain."

What causes a rainbow?

A rainbow is a colored arc that appears during or immediately after a rainshower. It is caused by the sun shining on the drops of rain.

A ray of sunlight does not pass directly through raindrops. Instead, the ray bends as it goes through drops of water, and is separated into the different colors that make up light. Each one bends at a different angle, forming a band of color. This gives us the multicolored arc that we call a rainbow. The colors are: violet, indigo, blue, green, yellow, orange and red. The larger the raindrops in the air, the more spectacular the rainbow will be.

What is hail?

Hail is a type of precipitation. Instead of falling as rain or snow, water droplets become coated with ice. Hailstones can be as small as a pea or as big as a baseball!

A hailstone is made in the clouds when ice crystals cling to drops of very cold water. Coatings of ice continue to form around the cold water droplet until the air currents in the cloud can no longer support the weight of the ice crystals. Then they fall to the ground as hail. Severe hailstorms can cause great damage to crops, animals, equipment, buildings and people.

Why isn't the weather forecaster always right?

Do you ever listen to the weather reports? A lot of the time the weather announcer's advice helps you dress to suit the weather. But sometimes the announcer is wrong. Have you ever been caught in the rain on a day that was supposed to be sunny?

Why isn't the weather forecaster always right? Actually, when you think of it, it is amazing that we can predict the weather as accurately as we do. For hundreds of years, people could not predict the weather. Then they started to examine the world around them and look for clues.

Now we have many ways of measuring the changes in the atmosphere. We measure air temperature with a thermometer, wind direction with a weather vane, atmospheric pressure with a barometer, wind speed with an anenometer, and humidity with a hygrometer. We even have radar to track and locate storms, and

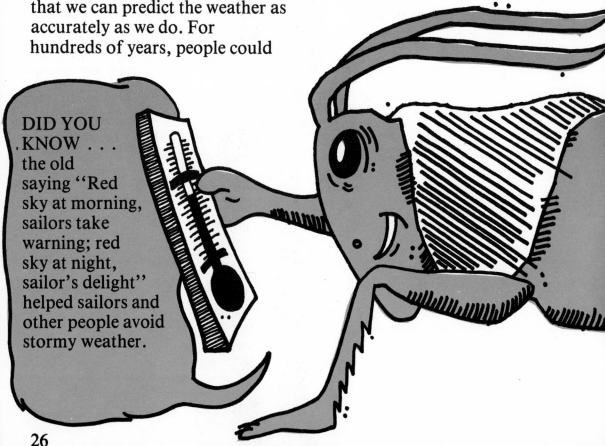

DID YOU KNOW . . . the old saying "Red sky at morning, sailors take warning; red sky at night, sailor's delight" helped sailors and other people avoid stormy weather.

satellites to scan the earth's surface and send down a picture of it.

But we still do not completely understand weather. Even with all the tools we have to tell us about weather conditions, there are still mysterious movements of air and temperature changes.

Until we learn more, we should be glad that the forecasts are right as often as they are!

Can animals predict the weather?

People used to believe that animals and birds could predict the weather. This is not true. Squirrels do not collect more nuts and deer do not grow thicker fur than usual before an extra cold winter. Birds do not roost before a storm.

But even if animals can't predict weather, crickets can tell temperature. Crickets chirp faster as the temperature rises. Some people say that counting the number of chirps in 15 seconds, and adding 37, will give you the temperature in Fahrenheit. Try it!

What is acid rain?

Acid rain is a type of pollution. When smoke from factory chimneys mixes with moisture in the atmosphere, it produces chemicals that can be as acidic as vinegar. These chemicals then fall to the earth when it rains.

Acid rain is dangerous for all living things in lakes as well as for trees and plants. It also contaminates drinking water and eats away at buildings.

Many people have become very concerned about this threat to the environment. As a result, there are now regulations forcing industries to clean up the exhaust they send into the air.

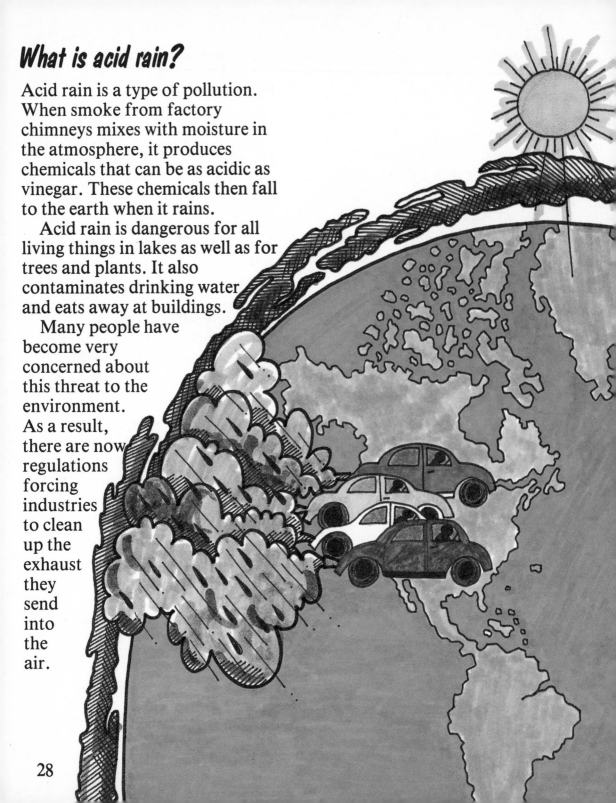

What is the greenhouse effect?

A greenhouse is made of glass. The sun's heat shines through the glass, but once inside, the heat cannot escape easily. Inside the greenhouse it is much warmer than outdoors. For this reason, people build greenhouses to grow plants that need warm temperatures.

The various gases that surround the earth act like the glass of a greenhouse: they let the heat of the sun in but keep it from returning to outer space. This means that the earth doesn't get too hot during the day or too cold during the night.

Scientists say the fumes from cars, furnaces and factories will cause the world's natural greenhouse to become too efficient. As a result, the world's weather will get warmer and warmer. That might be welcome on a cold winter's day, but think how unbearable summer might get!

This warming trend could eventually cause ice in the polar regions to melt, resulting in serious flooding. To avoid these dangers, we must limit the amount of chemical fumes we release into the air.

Does the weather affect our moods?

Some consequences of weather are well known. Weather can cause flooding or provide a beautiful sunny day. But how else can weather affect us?

Scientists believe that ions— tiny electrically charged particles of water that exist in the atmosphere—may affect our moods. When there are more negative ions in the air, people seem to be happier.

The high humidity which occurs during a storm makes some people irritable. Once the storm passes, moods return to normal.

Wind can also alter moods. The "vent du Midi" in southern France is said to cause headaches, and a hot, dry wind in North Africa is thought to make people depressed.

But the effects of weather on moods are not all negative. Warm temperatures and sunshine make many people feel cheerful and relaxed. Crisp, clear days in the fall and early winter encourage feelings of contentment and excitement.

The number of hours of daylight also influences moods. The increased hours of light in the summer make people happy and optimistic. Fewer hours of daylight in winter cause many people to feel sluggish and depressed. Some people take holidays in the winter to warm southern places to get more hours of sunshine and daylight.

Does a rain dance bring rain?

In ancient times, people built huge bonfires to try to please the gods so they would make it rain. In North America the native Indians performed elaborate rain dances that could last for up to several days. And sometimes rain would follow, as sometimes it does today when farmers in drought stricken areas pray for rain.

But did the dancing bring the rain? No one knows for certain why weather conditions change although there are many theories. Many people believe that faith and prayer—whatever form it takes—can make things happen. And no one has ever been able to prove they are wrong.

Index _____